STATE PROFILES

WASHINGTON

BY REBECCA SABELKO

BELLWETHER MEDIA • MINNEAPOLIS, MN

Blastoff! Discovery launches a new mission: reading to learn. Filled with facts and features, each book offers you an exciting new world to explore!

This edition first published in 2022 by Bellwether Media, Inc.

No part of this publication may be reproduced in whole or in part without written permission of the publisher.
For information regarding permission, write to Bellwether Media, Inc.,
Attention: Permissions Department,
6012 Blue Circle Drive, Minnetonka, MN 55343.

Library of Congress Cataloging-in-Publication Data

Names: Sabelko, Rebecca, author.
Title: Washington / by Rebecca Sabelko.
Description: Minneapolis, MN : Bellwether Media, Inc., 2022. |
   Series: Blastoff! Discovery: State profiles | Includes bibliographical
   references and index. | Audience: Ages 7-13 | Audience: Grades
   4-6 | Summary: "Engaging images accompany information about
   Washington. The combination of high-interest subject matter and
   narrative text is intended for students in grades 3 through 8"
   – Provided by publisher.
Identifiers: LCCN 2021020850 (print) | LCCN 2021020851 (ebook)
   | ISBN 9781644873533 (library binding) |
   ISBN 9781648341960 (ebook)
Subjects: LCSH: Washington (State)–Juvenile literature.
Classification: LCC F891.3 .S24 2022 (print) | LCC F891.3 (ebook)
   | DDC 979.7–dc23
LC record available at https://lccn.loc.gov/2021020850
LC ebook record available at https://lccn.loc.gov/2021020851

Editor: Colleen Sexton   Designer: Laura Sowers

Printed in the United States of America, North Mankato, MN.

TABLE OF CONTENTS

PIKE PLACE MARKET

PIKE PLACE MARKET

It is a bright Saturday morning in Seattle. A family heads to Pike Place Market. The joyful music of **buskers** fills the air. The family's first stop is the fish market. They watch workers throw fish to entertain the crowd. Next, the family heads to the colorful produce stands. They pick up ingredients to make dinner.

4

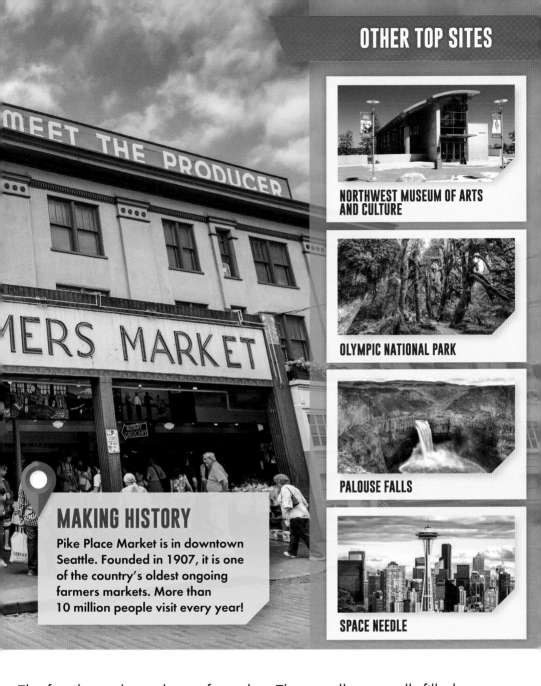

MEET THE PRODUCER

MERS MARKET

OTHER TOP SITES

NORTHWEST MUSEUM OF ARTS AND CULTURE

OLYMPIC NATIONAL PARK

PALOUSE FALLS

SPACE NEEDLE

MAKING HISTORY

Pike Place Market is in downtown Seattle. Founded in 1907, it is one of the country's oldest ongoing farmers markets. More than 10 million people visit every year!

The family explores the craft market. They stroll past stalls filled with handmade treasures. Their last stop is Rachel the Piggy Bank. Everyone drops a quarter into the slot. They rub her snout for luck. Pike Place Market is one of Washington's many special treats!

CANADA

STRAIT OF
JUAN DE FUCA

OLYMPIC
PENINSULA

PUGET
SOUND

WASHINGTON

● SEATTLE

● TACOMA

★ OLYMPIA

PACIFIC
OCEAN

COLUMBIA RIVER

OREGON

Washington is in the **Pacific Northwest** region of the United States. Canada is the state's northern neighbor. Idaho lies to the east. The Columbia River rushes along much of the southern border with Oregon. The Pacific Ocean washes the west coast. The **Strait** of Juan de Fuca cuts into the shoreline to create the Olympic **Peninsula**.

Washington covers 71,298 square miles (184,661 square kilometers). The capital city of Olympia is in western Washington. It sits at the southern tip of Puget **Sound**. Seattle and Tacoma are other major cities in this area. Spokane is a large city in the east.

Humans arrived in the Pacific Northwest thousands of years ago. Over time, they formed Native American tribes. The Quileute, Chinook, and other tribes settled on the coast. The Spokane, Okanogan, and other tribes in the east were **nomads**.

In 1775, Spanish explorers arrived on the Olympic Peninsula. They were searching for a water route to the Atlantic Ocean. British and American fur traders established posts into the early 1800s. Americans moved west toward Washington in the 1800s to farm and build industries. Washington became the 42nd state in 1889.

NATIVE PEOPLES OF WASHINGTON

TULALIP TRIBES OF WASHINGTON

- Original lands in the Cascade Mountains, from Vancouver Island in the north to Oregon in the south
- More than 4,900 in Washington today

THE CONFEDERATED TRIBES OF THE COLVILLE RESERVATION

- Original lands in eastern Washington and parts of Oregon, Idaho, and British Columbia, Canada
- Around 9,500 live in Washington today

THE CONFEDERATED TRIBES AND BANDS OF THE YAKAMA NATION

- Original lands in central Washington
- More than 30,000 on the Yakama Nation Reservation today

In western Washington, forests cover the Olympic Mountains on the Olympic Peninsula. The peaks become hills near the Columbia River to the south. Lowlands surround Puget Sound. Moving east, the land rises into the **volcanic** Cascade Mountains. They stretch through central Washington. The Cascades include Mount Rainier. It is the state's highest point. In the southeast, the Snake River flows through farmland in the Columbia **Plateau**.

SNAKE RIVER

MOUNT RAINIER

- OLYMPIC MOUNTAINS
- CASCADE MOUNTAINS
- COLUMBIA PLATEAU

N W E S

MOUNT SAINT HELENS

MOUNT SAINT HELENS

Mount Saint Helens erupted in 1980. It was the most destructive volcanic eruption in U.S. history. The volcano is still active today. But scientists believe it will not erupt for another 100 to 300 years.

SEASONAL HIGHS AND LOWS

SPRING
HIGH: 60°F (16°C)
LOW: 39°F (4°C)

SUMMER
HIGH: 78°F (26°C)
LOW: 52°F (11°C)

FALL
HIGH: 61°F (16°C)
LOW: 40°F (4°C)

WINTER
HIGH: 43°F (6°C)
LOW: 30°F (-1°C)

°F = degrees Fahrenheit
°C = degrees Celsius

PUGET SOUND

The Pacific Ocean and the state's mountain ranges affect much of Washington's climate. Western skies are often cloudy. Fog and rain are common year-round. East of the mountains, winters are cold and summers are warm.

11

Washington's wildlife is **diverse**. Seals sunbathe on the rocky shores of Puget Sound. Orcas feed in the sound's waters. In the Olympic Mountains, marmots whistle when bobcats are near. Bats hide in thick forests in the Cascades. Mountain goats perch on rocky slopes.

Spotted frogs and whipsnakes live in Washington's wetlands. Mallard ducks and Canada geese gather in lakes and streams. Eagles nest in the branches of evergreen trees along the Columbia River. They swoop down to pull salmon from the water.

ORCA

STRIPED WHIPSNAKE

HARBOR SEAL

BALD EAGLE

COLUMBIA SPOTTED FROG

OLYMPIC MARMOT

Life Span: up to 6 years
Status: least concern

Olympic marmot range = ■

LEAST CONCERN	NEAR THREATENED	VULNERABLE	ENDANGERED	CRITICALLY ENDANGERED	EXTINCT IN THE WILD	EXTINCT

Washington is home to more than 7 million people. Nine out of ten Washingtonians live in **urban** areas. More than half of the population resides in the cities of Seattle, Tacoma, and Bellevue.

JAPANESE PRISON CAMPS

Beginning in the 1890s, many Japanese immigrants made Washington their home. But in 1941, Japan attacked the United States during World War II. The U.S. government then forced many Japanese Americans into prison camps.

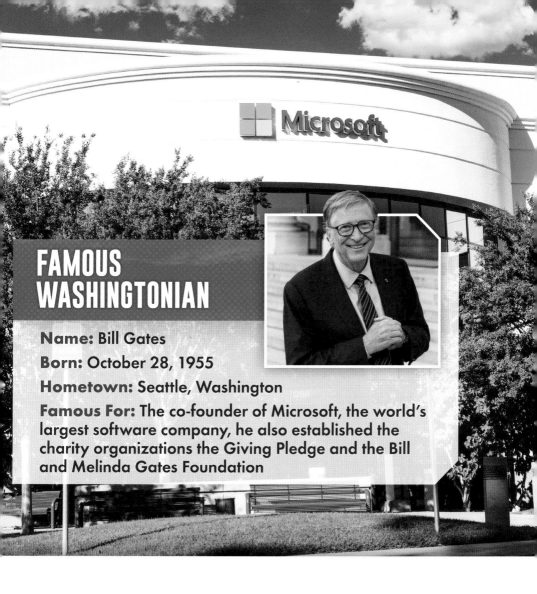

FAMOUS WASHINGTONIAN

Name: Bill Gates

Born: October 28, 1955

Hometown: Seattle, Washington

Famous For: The co-founder of Microsoft, the world's largest software company, he also established the charity organizations the Giving Pledge and the Bill and Melinda Gates Foundation

Around 4 out of every 5 Washingtonians have **ancestors** from England, Ireland, Germany, and other European nations. About 1 in 10 Washingtonians is Hispanic. The state has one of the country's largest populations of Asian Americans and Native Americans. Many of Washington's Native Americans live on the state's 29 **reservations**. Newcomers to Washington have arrived from Mexico, India, China, the Philippines, and Vietnam.

Founded in 1869, Seattle is Washington's largest city. It is also one of the country's fastest-growing cities. Seattle is home to many of the nation's largest companies. They include Microsoft and Amazon. The Port of Seattle is the sixth-busiest seaport in the United States. Trade goods from Asia arrive daily.

Residents enjoy biking, walking on the beach, and playing games at Discovery Park. They explore exhibits at the Museum of Pop Culture and the Museum of History and Industry. The towering Space Needle sparks adventure in residents and tourists. It offers views of downtown, surrounding mountains, and Puget Sound.

WASHINGTON'S CHALLENGE: HOUSING COSTS

Seattle is one of the country's most expensive places to live. The city also has one of the highest rates of homelessness. Groups are working to create affordable housing. They want to make living in the city an option for everyone.

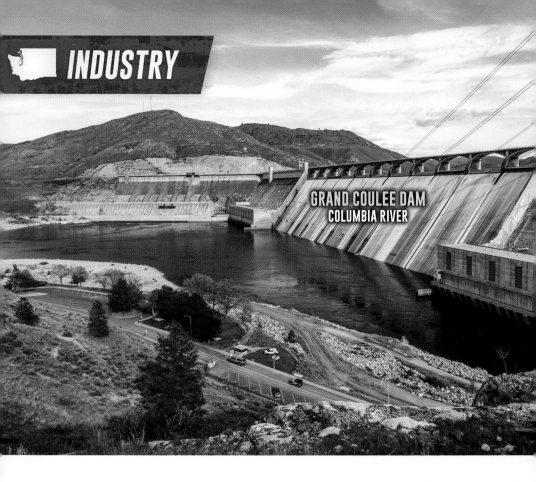

GRAND COULEE DAM
COLUMBIA RIVER

Washington's **natural resources** helped create successful industries. Around three-fourths of the state's forests support lumber production. The Grand Coulee Dam on the Columbia River is one of the world's largest power plants. Washington's rich soil produces wheat, potatoes, and asparagus. Farmers grow more apples and pears in Washington than in any other state. Washington is a leading fishing state. Crews pull salmon, halibut, and cod from coastal waters.

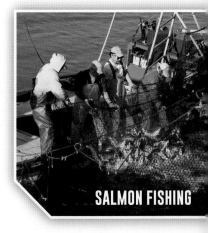

SALMON FISHING

Factory workers package seafood, fruit, and vegetables. Aircraft, shipbuilding, and computer industries provide more **manufacturing** jobs. Most Washingtonians have **service jobs**. They work in health care and the government. Tourism employs many hotel and restaurant workers.

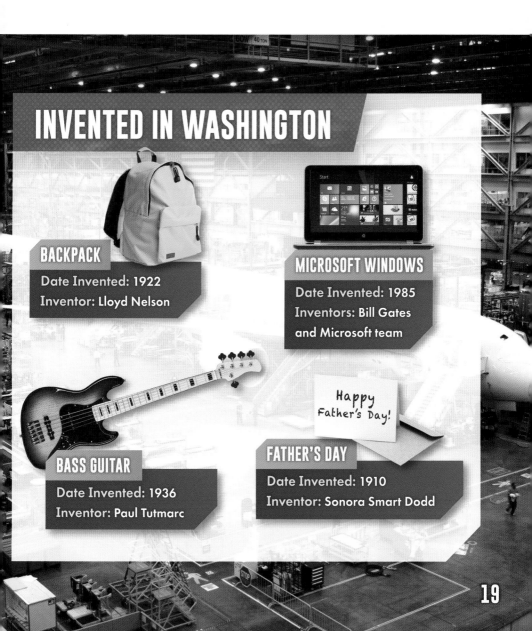

INVENTED IN WASHINGTON

BACKPACK
Date Invented: 1922
Inventor: Lloyd Nelson

MICROSOFT WINDOWS
Date Invented: 1985
Inventors: Bill Gates and Microsoft team

Happy Father's Day!

BASS GUITAR
Date Invented: 1936
Inventor: Paul Tutmarc

FATHER'S DAY
Date Invented: 1910
Inventor: Sonora Smart Dodd

FISH AND CHIPS

OYSTER STEW

Washingtonians enjoy fresh seafood all year. Smoked or grilled salmon is a favorite. Fish and chips appear on local menus. Oysters, razor clams, and geoduck clams are served raw on the half shell. Washingtonians fill bowls with oyster stew and clam chowder.

Korean **immigrants** introduced grilled teriyaki chicken, beef, and pork. Cooks serve up the popular Vietnamese soup *pho*. It features a spiced beef broth, rice noodles, meat, and vegetables. For dessert, bakers fill pies with apples and cherries. A favorite sweet treat is Canadian Nanaimo bars. They feature layers of chocolate, custard, and graham crackers.

WALLA WALLA SWEET ONIONS

Walla Walla sweet onions are the state vegetable. They often top sandwiches and burgers. Some people bite into whole Walla Wallas. They eat them like apples!

APPLESAUCE

16 SERVINGS

Have an adult help you make this tasty dish!

INGREDIENTS

about 16 tart apples, peeled and sliced
1 cup apple juice
1 teaspoon cinnamon
1/2 teaspoon allspice
1/2 teaspoon cloves

DIRECTIONS

1. Combine all the ingredients into a large Dutch oven or pot. Bring to a boil.

2. Reduce heat, cover, and simmer for 25 to 35 minutes or until the apples are soft. Stir occasionally.

3. Remove from heat and mash the apples. Serve warm or cold!

CAMPING IN NORTH CASCADES
NATIONAL PARK

Washingtonians enjoy the state's beautiful landscapes year-round. They head to the state's many mountain peaks to ski and snowboard in cold weather. The state's three national parks welcome hikers and campers in summer and fall. Boaters flock to Puget Sound to enjoy water sports and fishing.

SNOWBOARDING

Washingtonians cheer for professional football, basketball, soccer, baseball, and hockey teams. The state is also well known for its music and art scenes. The award-winning Seattle Symphony performs beautiful music. The Pratt Fine Arts Center welcomes everyone to share their creativity!

SEATTLE SYMPHONY

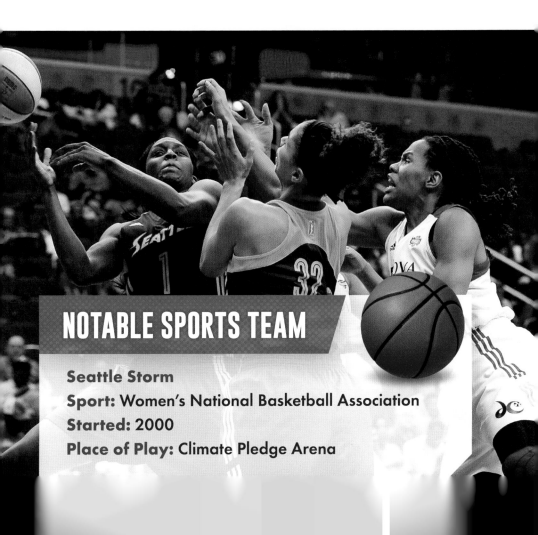

NOTABLE SPORTS TEAM

Seattle Storm
Sport: Women's National Basketball Association
Started: 2000
Place of Play: Climate Pledge Arena

FESTIVALS AND TRADITIONS

SEAFAIR

BUMBERSHOOT

Many Washingtonians gather for Seafair in Seattle. This summer festival includes a torchlight parade, boat races, and air shows. Bumbershoot is one of the country's biggest art festivals. Visitors enjoy live music, comedy acts, dance, and films.

Spokane hosts the Northwest Winterfest from November to January. Crowds celebrate holiday **traditions** from around the world. The festival features painted Chinese lanterns, Irish dance performances, and Philippine bamboo stick dancing. Tacoma throws an exciting First Night party to ring in the New Year. Music and dance performances, a parade, and fireworks make it a special night. There is so much to celebrate in the great state of Washington!

SKAGIT VALLEY TULIP FESTIVAL

A SPRING OF COLOR

Each April, the Skagit Valley Tulip Festival celebrates the blooming of millions of tulips. Visitors also enjoy trolley rides, face painting, and kite flying!

1853

The Washington Territory is created, with land including all of present-day Washington and parts of Idaho and Montana

1775

Explorer Bruno de Hezeta lands on the Olympic Peninsula and claims the area for Spain

1885

The U.S. government forces the Nez Percé to move to the Colville Indian Reservation

1889

Washington becomes a state

1805

The Lewis and Clark expedition enters the area that is now Washington

1910

Women gain the right to vote in Washington

1941

The Grand Coulee Dam is completed

1980

Mount Saint Helens erupts

2014

The Seattle Seahawks win their first Super Bowl

1979

Microsoft moves its headquarters to Washington

Nicknames: The Evergreen State, The Chinook State

Motto: *Alki* (a Chinook word meaning "by and by")

Date of Statehood: November 11, 1889
(the 42nd state)

Capital City: Olympia ★

Other Major Cities: Seattle, Spokane, Tacoma, Vancouver

Area: 71,298 square miles (184,661 square kilometers);
Washington is the 18th largest state.

Population

7,705,281
(2020)

STATE FLAG

Adopted in 1923, Washington's flag is green with the state seal in the center. The seal features George Washington, the first president of the United States, on a blue background. The gold border circling the seal includes the year of statehood, 1889. It also includes the words "The seal of the state of Washington."

INDUSTRY

Main Exports

 oil

 soybeans

 wheat

 medical equipment

 corn

 aircraft parts

JOBS

- MANUFACTURING **7%**
- FARMING AND NATURAL RESOURCES **4%**
- GOVERNMENT **15%**
- SERVICES **74%**

Natural Resources
rich soil, timber, water

GOVERNMENT

Federal Government

10 REPRESENTATIVES | **2** SENATORS

WA

12 ELECTORAL VOTES

USA

State Government

98 REPRESENTATIVES | **49** SENATORS

STATE SYMBOLS

STATE BIRD
WILLOW GOLDFINCH

STATE OCEAN ANIMAL
ORCA

STATE FLOWER
COAST RHODODENDRON

STATE TREE
WESTERN HEMLOCK

ancestors—relatives who lived long ago

buskers—people who entertain in a public place

diverse—made up of people or things that are different from one another

immigrants—people who move to a new country

manufacturing—a field of work in which people use machines to make products

natural resources—materials in the earth that are taken out and used to make products or fuel

nomads—people who have no fixed home but wander from place to place

Pacific Northwest—an area of the United States that includes Washington, Oregon, and Idaho

peninsula—a section of land that extends out from a larger piece of land and is almost completely surrounded by water

plateau—an area of flat, raised land

reservations—areas of land that are controlled by Native American tribes

service jobs—jobs that perform tasks for people or businesses

sound—a long waterway separating a mainland and an island or connecting two larger bodies of water

strait—a narrow channel connecting two large bodies of water

tourists—people who travel to visit another place

traditions—customs, ideas, or beliefs handed down from one generation to the next

urban—related to cities and city life

volcanic—relating to volcanoes; a volcano is a hole in the earth that erupts hot ash, gas, or melted rock called lava.

AT THE LIBRARY

Johnson, Anna Maria. *Washington*. New York, N.Y.: Cavendish Square, 2020.

McDaniel, Melissa. *Washington*. New York, N.Y.: Children's Press, 2019.

Rusch, Elizabeth. *Will It Blow? Become a Volcano Detective at Mount St. Helens*. Seattle, Wash.: Sasquatch Books, 2017.

ON THE WEB

FACTSURFER

Factsurfer.com gives you a safe, fun way to find more information.

1. Go to www.factsurfer.com.

2. Enter "Washington" into the search box and click 🔍.

3. Select your book cover to see a list of related content.

INDEX